Round the World

The Journey of Tania Aebi

Rebecca Weber

PACIFIC
LEARNING

© 2004 **Pacific Learning**
© 2004 Written by **Rebecca Weber**
Edited by **Alison Auch**
Designed by **Anna-Maria Crum**
Photography courtesy of **Tania Aebi**
Additional photography: NASA, pp. 11, 37

The author would like to give special thanks to Tania Aebi for providing her story and for sharing her photographs, without which this book would never have happened.

08 07 06 05 04
10 9 8 7 6 5 4 3 2 1

Published by
Pacific Learning
P.O. Box 2723
Huntington Beach, CA 92647-0723
www.pacificlearning.com

ISBN: 1-59055-390-X
PL-7412

Printed in China.

Contents

Introduction

What makes an adventurer? Most people see a classic adventurer as a large, strong man, braving new lands and seeking riches or fame. Sometimes, the true definition of an adventurer couldn't be more different.

Once, not too many years ago, a brave eighteen-year-old girl left behind her life in the big city and began a death-defying journey.

It all started with a **challenge** from her dad.

Tania and her father, Ernst Aebi

New York City

Tania Aebi, a young girl from New York City, was struggling to figure out what to do with her life. She'd left both her home and high school a few years before, and was working as a bicycle messenger. She knew she didn't want to go to college, but she also knew that she was ready for a new challenge.

Tania's father was equally worried about Tania's future. He'd spent his life following daring dreams, and he feared that his oldest child might get into trouble, or – even more frightening to him – do nothing with her life.

Then, in 1983, Tania's father developed an interest in sailing, and as always, Ernst Aebi followed his new hobby with all his heart. He bought a sailboat in England, and invited his children to help him crew the boat on a journey to the Canary Islands.

After only three days of training, Tania found herself on the ocean for the first time. Before she knew what was happening, Tania was hooked. On her second trip, somewhere in the middle of the Atlantic Ocean, her father came up with a plan.

Tania with her father and sister Nina

Since Tania wasn't interested in going to college, what if he took her college money and instead bought her a sailboat? Then, she could have an adventure of her own.

Ernst's idea was for Tania to sail around the world... and to make it interesting, she'd need to do it by herself.

Before she knew it, Tania's journey started to fall into place. For months she and her father searched for the perfect boat, finally finding it at a boat show: a tiny sailboat named *Varuna*, which was 26 feet (7.9 m) long, and only $7^1/_2$ feet (2.3 m) wide.

Tania Aebi

Getting Tania and *Varuna* ready for the trip took a great deal of planning. Tania took a course in how to **navigate** using the stars as a guide. She and her father shopped for the supplies she would need to stay alive, and to keep her boat in good working order.

Most important, Tania searched for a way to say good-bye to her friends and family. She knew this would be more difficult than any dangers she would encounter during the days ahead.

Alone on the Atlantic

May 30, 1985: Departure Day

The day Tania left New York was a blur of TV and newspaper interviews. After hours of flashing cameras, and questions that made her even more nervous, Tania and *Varuna* finally motored out of the harbor in late afternoon.

Sailing away from New York

Tania was exhausted. She steered the boat toward a small cove, and once *Varuna* was safely anchored, Tania fell fast asleep.

The next morning, things looked much brighter. Some people on a neighboring boat invited her for breakfast, and Tania soon set off on the first leg of her journey to Bermuda.

Unfortunately, Tania had never had a chance to take *Varuna* out into the ocean before, and when the boat hit open water, seawater started to rush in. Tania quickly found the source of her problem, and packed the leak with shopping bags and duct tape.

"Varuna" under sail

She was glad she'd been able to solve her first real emergency so easily. Still, it left her nervous, and a little worried.

On this first leg of her journey, Tania's engine stopped working, she faced her first waves and wind from a major storm, and worried constantly about getting lost.

Finally, after nearly two weeks at sea, Tania and *Varuna* limped into Bermuda. She now had a good idea about how dangerous this trip was going to be.

Tania's father flew down to Bermuda to help her make some much needed repairs. Soon Tania was ready to tackle the next stage of her journey.

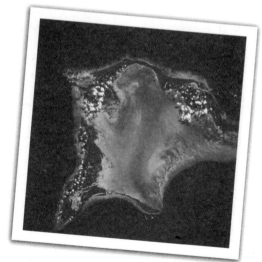

A bird's-eye view of Bermuda

For days, there was no real wind, and *Varuna* baked under the summer sun. Finally the trade winds kicked in, and Tania sped toward the island of St. Thomas. When she arrived, she was tired. Her sister Jade flew down to join her, and together they celebrated the Fourth of July.

Meanwhile, Jade had brought a very important present to Tania – a cat! Tania named him Dinghy, and was thrilled that she would now have a friend for the long, lonely voyages across the open sea.

Dinghy

Soon it was time to leave again. Tania and her father had figured out that if she completed the trip by November of 1987, she'd break the world record. Tania had a schedule to keep, and her next stop was the Panama Canal.

Panama Canal

After another nine days of sailing, Tania found herself at the canal. To learn how to get through the dangerous **locks**, Tania agreed to crew for another boat that was going through. She quickly became friends with Luc and Jean Marie, the two Frenchmen who were on this boat, and in turn, they helped her sail *Varuna* through to the Pacific Ocean.

A New Ocean

In August of 1985, Tania and her new friends anchored their boats at Taboga Island, off the coast of Panama. Together, they basked in the peaceful waters that had given the Pacific Ocean its name hundreds of years before.

One day, when Luc and Jean Marie were fixing the engine on their boat, Tania swam under her boat to clean off the barnacles. Without warning, she was stung by an enormous jellyfish.

As Tania went into shock from the poison of the jellyfish, her new friends cared for her, covering the welts with clay powder and water.

After a few weeks, Tania felt ready to move on. The friends parted and began their separate journeys to the Galapagos Islands.

Halfway there, Tania's troublesome engine gave out yet again. She was now alone on the ocean, without radio or lights. Despite this, she managed to cross the equator, where she celebrated by opening packages from her family that she'd been saving for this special occasion.

Then, just days later, she found herself in the magical Galapagos Islands.

Even though the Galapagos were beautiful, Tania was starting to worry about crossing the Pacific Ocean during storm season. After only eleven days, she and her friends set off again on the 3,000-mile (4,828-km) trip to the Marquesas Islands – the longest journey yet.

In the Galapagos Islands

This trip terrified Tania. The ocean was so huge, and her boat so small.

For the next three and a half weeks, Tania battled the winds and the waves. October 7 was her nineteenth birthday, and she gladly opened the presents she'd been saving since New York, even though they made her homesick.

Finally, Tania and *Varuna* cruised into the Marquesas. During her telephone calls home, though, Tania heard terrible news. Her mother was dying.

Suddenly the plans changed, and Tania bought a plane ticket home from Tahiti, her next stop. After quickly restocking her boat, Tania set out for Tahiti. Oh this journey, the winds turned against her, and while her boat bobbed in windless seas, her airplane home flew across the sky above her.

Finally, Tania was able to get home, where she spent Christmas with her family. More importantly, she spent her final days with her mother.

Two days after Christmas, Tania flew back to Tahiti, to await the news of her mother's death, and to avoid the hurricane season.

She **grieved** and rested in the island paradise for the next four months.

Sleeping in the Pacific

During her time in Tahiti, Tania made some wonderful new friends, and even adopted a second cat named Mimine. Unfortunately, she also had to say good-bye to Luc and Jean Marie. Tania knew she needed to start sailing again, but couldn't bear to leave the safe island.

Finally, on Friday, April 28, 1986, Tania sailed away. She had heard the sailors' warnings about never beginning a journey on a Friday, but she didn't believe in the old myths.

Within hours, Tania had developed a terrible ear infection and was sailing into a a violent storm. Dizzy from pain, she fought to keep her boat upright during the four-day storm. Then she fell and sprained her wrist, making sail changes almost impossible.

The one and only fish Tania caught

Even after she landed in Samoa, the bad luck stayed with Tania. A friend of hers needed to get from one island to another, and Tania let her ride on *Varuna* for eighty miles (129 km). Weeks later, Tania received an unsigned note warning her that someone was going to report that she had traveled with another person. It would ruin Tania's record for sailing solo around the world.

Even worse, while docked at an island with some friends on another boat, the two boats crashed into one another, damaging *Varuna.*

Some of the people Tania met in the South Seas

Finally, on July 11, Tania's luck changed. She crossed the **International Date Line** on her journey to a South Seas island named Vanuatu.

While she was anchored in these islands, she went to a party on a nearby boat. There, she met a man from Switzerland named Olivier, who was sailing a boat named *Akka* around the world.

Within days, Tania and Olivier were **inseparable**. Together they explored the islands on their two boats. Before long, they'd adopted the local way of saying they belonged to each other: "I blong you."

As happy as Tania was, she was worried about her dear cat Dinghy. After sailing nearly halfway around the world with him, he'd been her best friend and constant companion. Suddenly he stopped eating, and one day he began bleeding.

Tania and Olivier rushed Dinghy to the veterinarian, who was not able to save him. Tania's brave little friend was dead. Desperately sad, Tania adopted another cat whom she named Tarzoon.

Looking out at Olivier's boat

Soon Tania knew that she needed to move on if she were going to keep to her increasingly tight schedule. With her two cats on board, she and Olivier sailed *Varuna* and *Akka* out of the South Seas islands. As they left, a pod of whales swam along with them, seeming to wish them a safe trip.

CHAPTER

3

Halfway to Home

As they sailed toward Australia, Tania and Olivier needed to make some decisions about their journey. They'd spent so much time in the South Seas that they were rapidly approaching the Indian Ocean's storm season. To survive the trip, they were going to need to travel fast.

Before anything else, however, they had to face the dangers of crossing the Great Barrier Reef that stood between them and Australia. With her sharp navigation skills, Tania found the one lighthouse that could guide her safely to land. Fighting stormy seas, she and *Varuna* made their way to shore.

All along, Tania had planned to travel from Australia down around the southern tip of Africa. Now she didn't have time for this trip if she hoped to make her deadline. She and Olivier were going to need to travel to Asia instead.

On the scorching trip to Bali, the winds died out altogether and Tania and Olivier suffered from the heat. On one of the hottest days, they heard boats approaching, and the Australian Coast Guard tossed boxes of ice cream over to their boats.

Mimine and Tarzoon

From the northern tip of Australia, Tania's route took her to Bali, and then to Christmas Island. As much as Tania and Olivier wanted to explore and enjoy the islands, hurricane season was approaching fast. They had to keep moving.

Still, Tania called the trip from Christmas Island the most beautiful part of her journey. Even though she'd lost sight of Olivier and Mimine – who was riding on his boat – early on, hundreds of dolphins swam alongside her.

As Tania sailed from Christmas Island to Sri Lanka, Christmas came and went. With only her cat as company, she opened presents from Olivier and her family.

A tea plantation in Sri Lanka

A statue of Buddha, Sri Lanka

The 1,800-mile (2,897-km) trip north across the equator was slow, and *Varuna* bobbed along in the **doldrums**, moving only a few miles a day.

Finally, on January 7, 1987, Tania approached Sri Lanka, off the coast of India. As she sailed into the busy shipping lanes, she was almost run down by freighters. Shouting into her radio, she tried to alert the ships that she was there.

Finally, exhausted after her month alone at sea, Tania and *Varuna* landed in Sri Lanka. Even though no one had known the exact time she'd arrive, there was a telephone call waiting for her.

Tania's father, worried by her many delays in arriving at port, was waiting to speak to her. It only took a few minutes of talking to convince him that he needed to travel to Sri Lanka to help Tania refit her battered boat.

After so many quiet days alone, Sri Lanka was bustling and amazing to Tania. Still, nothing was as powerful as seeing her father again after eighteen months apart. Tania was nervous about introducing her father to Olivier, but the two seemed to get along well.

Tania spent the next month working with her father and Olivier, and exploring Sri Lanka. Together, they prepared *Varuna* for the next, and perhaps most difficult, part of her journey – the 2,400-mile (3,862-km) trip across the Arabian Sea.

Several days after Tania and Olivier left Sri Lanka, they met up with huge waves. Tania didn't realize how bad they were and didn't take in her sails quickly enough. Within minutes, a huge wave knocked down her boat and flooded the cabin.

As they approached India, their boats were surrounded by pollution. Even worse, Tania was hit by a terrible case of food poisoning that kept her curled up on her bunk for days.

As huge ships barreled past, Tania realized that no one could see her. Each day, she worried that she and Tarzoon might have to abandon *Varuna* if the ship were ever run down.

A market in Sri Lanka

Finally, Tania and Olivier met up again in Djibouti, in Africa, and then started to sail north up the Red Sea on their way to Sudan, south of Egypt. They had escaped the dangerous hurricane season,

A mosque in Djibouti

but now faced the howling winds and busy shipping lanes of the Red Sea.

To drive home the point that sailing was as filled with danger as it was with beauty, a good friend of Tania and Olivier's was killed as he sailed behind them out of Djibouti. The **boom** of his ship had swung around and crashed into his head. Tania and Olivier didn't discover this until they landed in Sudan weeks later.

While they were in Port Sudan, Tania and
Olivier tried to see as much of Sudan as quickly
as they could. They went to a wedding, and even
saw the president of Sudan in a parade.

Still, Tania's travel deadline weighed on
them. It was already April, and they needed to
be moving on.

Some friendly Sudanese children

Sunset on the Red Sea

As Tania and Olivier sailed out of Port Sudan, the Red Sea's famed winds beat at them, howling around their heads and shredding their sails. Tania struggled with scissors, spare cloth, and rubber cement to try to patch her sails back together between the gusts of wind and high waves.

Finally, on June 14, Tania and Olivier sailed into Port Suez, in Egypt. After tearing up their boats, and causing constant sleeplessness and worry from the threat of other boats, the hated Red Sea was finally behind them.

Racing the Weather

As Tania pulled into port, there were two huge boxes waiting for her. Her father had sent new sails, a bright new light, a steering device, and tons of delicious food.

Tania needed all of these, but even more, she needed rest. She was skinny, ill, and exhausted after her battles with the Red Sea.

Unfortunately, there was no time in her tight schedule for resting up. If she hoped to cross the Atlantic Ocean before the storm season, she needed to keep moving.

Tarzoon

While Tania fixed up *Varuna*, she and Olivier met some new friends. These friends just loved Tania's cat Mimine and begged to adopt her. Tania agreed, so now it was just Tania and Tarzoon together for the rest of the journey.

As Tania pulled out of Port Suez to sail on to Malta, south of Italy, her worst fears came true. Once again she'd ignored the myths about starting a journey on a Friday, and once again she ran into trouble.

Tania had stepped out of the howling winds to warm up with a cup of coffee when a loud horn jolted her. She ran up, just in time to see a huge cargo ship coming right at her. With no time to do anything, Tania froze.

Somehow, some way, *Varuna* almost missed the cargo boat entirely, until one of its hanging pieces grabbed *Varuna's* **mast** and almost ripped it off.

Patching the boat together the best she could, she sailed on to Malta. There, she was surprised with a visit from her brother Tony.

Tania, Olivier, and Tony stayed in Malta for four weeks, once again repairing *Varuna.* Tania knew she had to be moving on, but she couldn't bear to leave because this was the last she'd see of Olivier, whose own round-the-world trip was now complete.

No winds to help sail

Finally, Tania knew she couldn't put off her journey another minute. Olivier loaded boxes of his treasured souvenirs into *Varuna,* and gave Tania presents to open along the way on her lonely journey home.

On August 22, Olivier untied *Varuna's* lines, and both crying, the pair shouted good-bye to each other. Tania was alone and **devastated**.

As Tania sailed across the Mediterranean, she couldn't rest because of her fears of the sea's busy shipping lanes. She managed to avoid the other ships by forcing herself to look out once an hour, day and night. She even avoided the horrible pollution, which seemed to pave the waters with plastics, logs, and barrels.

Still, she couldn't avoid the weather. A week after setting out, *Varuna* sailed into a terrible storm. Tania was so tired after her many sleepless nights that she wasn't as careful as usual, and didn't shut the hatch behind her when she went below.

Suddenly, a huge wave hit the boat so hard that *Varuna* almost rolled completely before righting itself. Tania and Tarzoon were thrown around, and many of Tania's possessions were washed away. Those she still had were spilled, **waterlogged**, and broken.

Tania's boat, which had seemed ready for the journey across the Atlantic Ocean, was in trouble. She needed help.

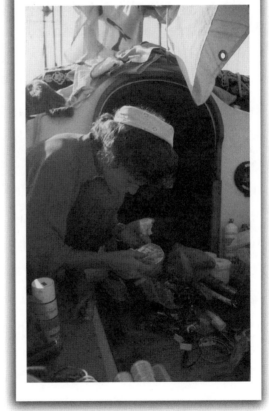

Cleaning up after the rollover

As Tania nursed *Varuna* to the closest port, she thought about giving up the journey. It was so difficult, so dangerous. Still, after a tearful call to her father, she crept back to her bunk and slept for several days straight. On waking, she thought she still might be able to make it.

When Tania finally got her boat to Gibraltar, her last stop before crossing the Atlantic, her father was waiting for her.

Once again, they worked to repair the little boat. And once again, after only a week, Tania had to say good-bye and sail off on her own.

The journey across the Atlantic was frightening for a few reasons. It was already mid-September, which was late in the season for sailing, and Tania knew the seas would be stormy. It was also going to be her longest trip, stretching more than 3,500 miles (5,633 km) before she'd see land again.

Tania faced storm after storm, with terrible winds and thirty-foot (nine-m) waves. Slowly, she and Tarzoon crossed the rough seas. She worried that she'd run out of food and water as the days slipped away.

On October 28, Tania crossed over the path that she'd taken two years before. Her **circumnavigation** was technically over. Now all she had to do was make it back to New York.

A satellite view of a weather front in the Atlantic Ocean

Homecoming!

November 6, 1987: Home at Last

After fifty days alone at sea, Tania and Tarzoon were sitting in the morning calm. Tania had just used her last few drops of fresh water to wash her face, and had put on her last pair of clean long johns to keep out the chilly air.

It was time to start the final few miles into New York Harbor, and Tania felt nervous. How much had changed while she was away? Would she ever fit in to her old life again?

Tania with "New York Post" headline

Tania and Olivier

As she began to sail for home, the morning's silence was broken by the roar of a loud powerboat. Suddenly journalists were shouting questions at her and people were taking her picture. Tania searched for a friendly face, but saw no one she knew.

Then, just a little while later, another powerboat pulled near. There, among the TV cameras, were her father and Olivier.

Over all the noise and confusion, Tania heard the words she'd shared so many times since meeting Olivier: "I blong you, Tania!"

She was home.

Despite the many delays and dangers, Tania Aebi had managed to become both the first American woman and the youngest person ever to sail around the world by herself.

Unfortunately, because of that one small eighty-mile (129-km) trip back in the South Seas, when she'd let a friend ride on her boat, she didn't get to set any official records.

Still, it was the accomplishment of a lifetime. She'd had exactly the adventure – and so much more – that her father had hoped she'd have.

The South Street Seaport, New York

Life Back on Land

Of course, much had changed at home since Tania was away. The biggest change was that she'd lost her mother to cancer. Another was that she had grown into a new life over the past few years.

When she'd left, she was a frightened, street-smart teenager. Now she was an adult, and she was ready to settle down to a new life.

Tania, Nora, Jade, and Tony

About a year after returning home, Tania and Olivier married, and moved away from the city's noise and pollution so that Tania could write.

Early on, Tania repaid her father by selling *Varuna.* She went to college, and went on to earn a master of fine arts in creative nonfiction writing. Still, she's never left sailing behind. Each year, she makes several voyages in which she teaches other women how to sail and navigate.

While she sailed around the world, Tania had earned money by writing articles for a sailing magazine. She also wrote an autobiography of her journey. To this day, Tania still writes a magazine column about sailing.

Tania's home in Vermont

Tania with Nicholas and Sam

More importantly, Tania has focused her
energies on her two sons, Nicholas and Sam.
Although she knows that they will need to live
their own lives, she shares with them one of the
major lessons she learned during her journey:
not to be scared of the world. She tells them to
be brave with people and to be open to people,
but always with their own eyes open.

More than fifteen years after her journey ended, Tania still feels the power of her great adventure. She says, "The trip places me historically. The ocean opened up the big picture of what life is and what it can be."

And as for that record that she didn't win because of giving a lift to a friend? Well, in the long run, it doesn't really matter. Breaking the record was never Tania's main goal.

Tania with navigation students

The trip and the accomplishments were the important parts, and no one will ever take that away from her!

Tania with Tarzoon, who is still alive!

The Journey around the World

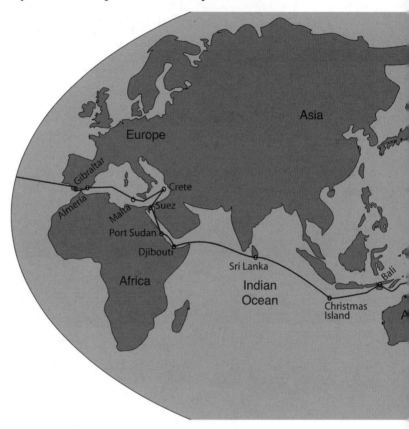

New York – Bermuda
  5/30 – 6/12/85
Bermuda – St. Thomas
  6/20 – 7/1/85
St. Thomas – Panama
  7/17 – 7/27/85
Panama – Galapagos
  9/1 – 9/18/85
Galapagos – Marquesas
  9/29 – 10/23/85
Marquesas – Tahiti
  11/28 – 12/6/85

Moorea – Samoa
  5/9/86 – 5/27/86
Samoa – Wallis
  6/21 – 6/23/86
Wallis – Futuna
  7/7 – 7/8/86
Futuna – Vanuavatu
  7/10 – 7/17/86
Vanuavatu – Cairns
  8/21 – 9/4/86

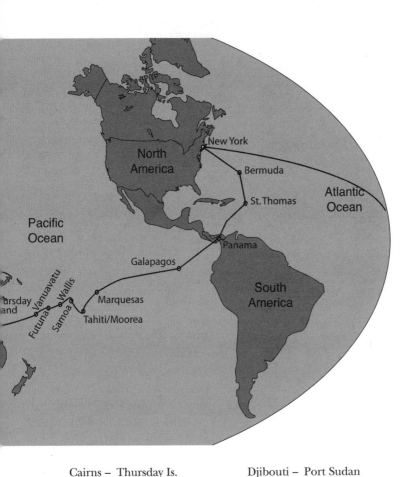

Cairns – Thursday Is.
9/19 – 10/10/86
Thursday Is. – Bali
10/20 – 11/20/86
Bali – Christmas Is.
11/27 – 12/2/86
Christmas Is. – Sri Lanka
12/8/86 – 1/8/87
Sri Lanka – Djibouti
2/10 – 3/9/87

Djibouti – Port Sudan
3/24 – 4/6/87
Port Sudan – Suez
4/30 – 7/3/87
Suez – Crete – Malta
7/3 – 7/24/87
Malta – Gibraltar
8/22 – 9/8/87
Gibraltar – New York
9/16 – 11/6/87

Index

Glossary

boom – the long, thin pole that swings back and forth from the mast, and that the bottom edge of a sail attaches to

challenge – something that is difficult or frightening

circumnavigation – a trip that goes all the way around the world

devastated – desperately sad, with feelings of hopelessness

doldrums – a time of little or no wind, very calm

grieve – to feel sad, especially following a death

inseparable – unwilling to be apart for any length of time

International Date Line – an imaginary line in the Pacific Ocean that runs from the North Pole to the South Pole, and which is considered the place that each calendar day begins

lock – a canal that has gates at each end, which when closed can raise or lower a boat, so it can connect to another waterway

mast – the tall, upright pole that the sail attaches to

navigate – to find one's way around something

waterlogged – soaked with water